32 Reasons to Love Ireland
A Guide to the Country's 32 Counties

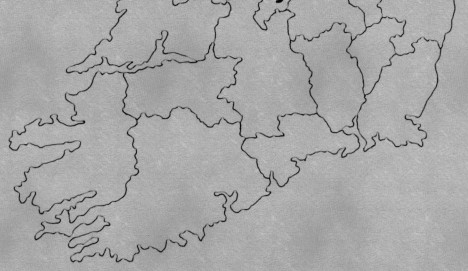

Dazelle designs

Contents

Éire

Ireland

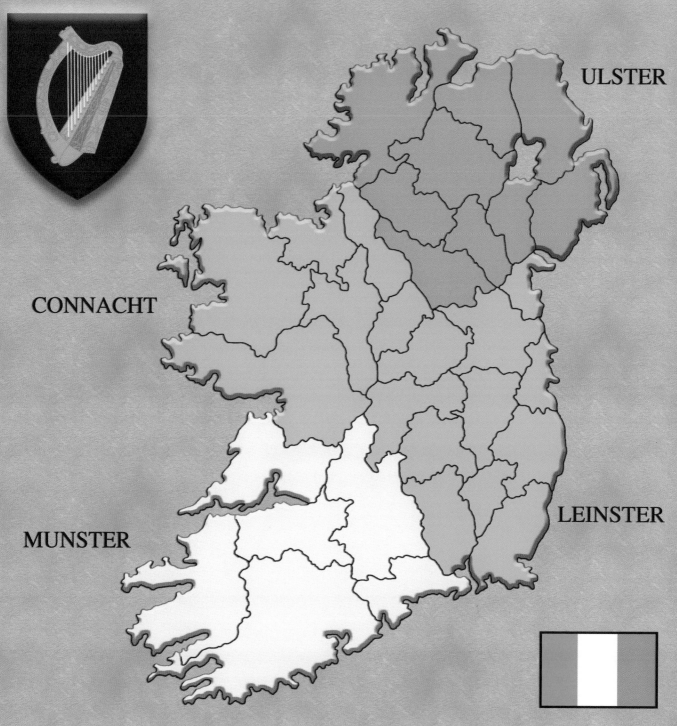

ULSTER

CONNACHT

LEINSTER

MUNSTER

**Ireland is an island nation located in northwestern Europe,
known for its rich history, stunning landscapes, and friendly people.
It is divided into four provinces:
Ulster, Leinster, Munster, and Connacht, and 32 counties.**

Ulster

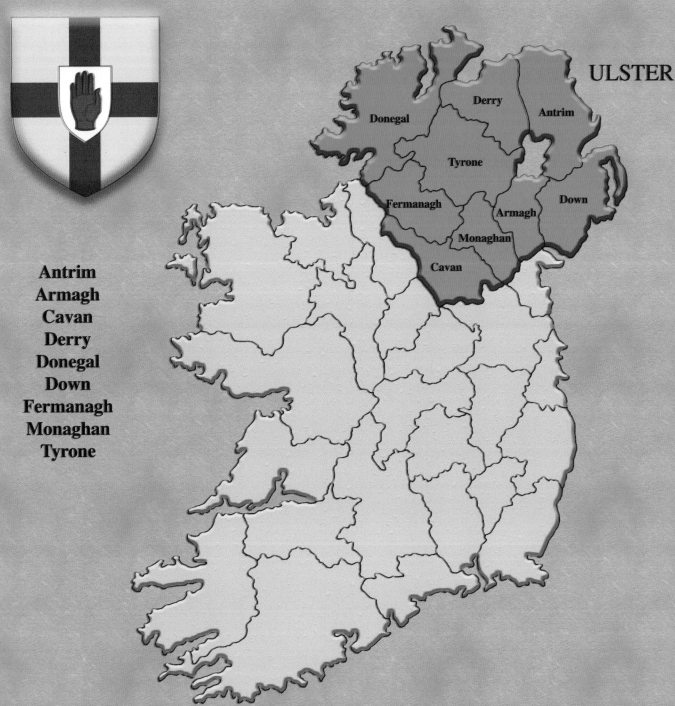

ULSTER

Antrim
Armagh
Cavan
Derry
Donegal
Down
Fermanagh
Monaghan
Tyrone

Ulster is a province located in the northern part of the island of Ireland.
It is composed of nine counties. Ulster is known for its rugged landscape,
rich history, and cultural traditions, including music, dance, and language.

Leinster

Carlow
Dublin
Kildare
Kilkenny
Laois
Longford
Louth
Meath
Offaly
Westmeath
Wexford
Wicklow

Longford · Louth · Meath · Westmeath · Offaly · Dublin · Kildare · Laois · Wicklow · Carlow · Kilkenny · Wexford

LEINSTER

Leinster is a province located in the eastern part of the island of Ireland.
It is the most populous province in the country and is home to the capital city of Dublin,
which is also the largest city in Ireland. Leinster is known for its vibrant cities
and towns, rich history, and stunning natural scenery, which includes the
Wicklow Mountains and the Boyne Valley.

Munster

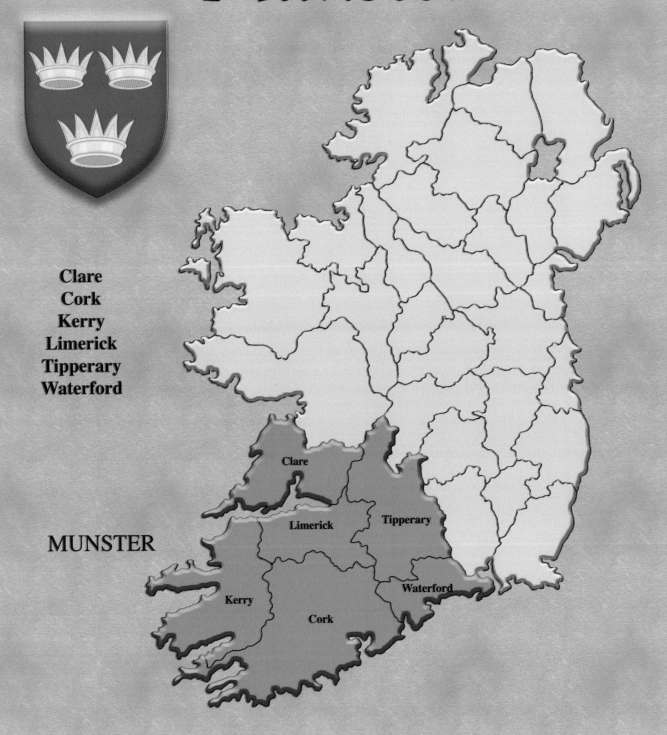

Clare
Cork
Kerry
Limerick
Tipperary
Waterford

MUNSTER

Munster is located in the southern part of the country.
Munster is known for its stunning natural landscapes, including the Ring of Kerry and
the Cliffs of Moher, as well as its rich cultural heritage, ancient castles and ruins,
and historic cities like Cork and Limerick.

Connacht

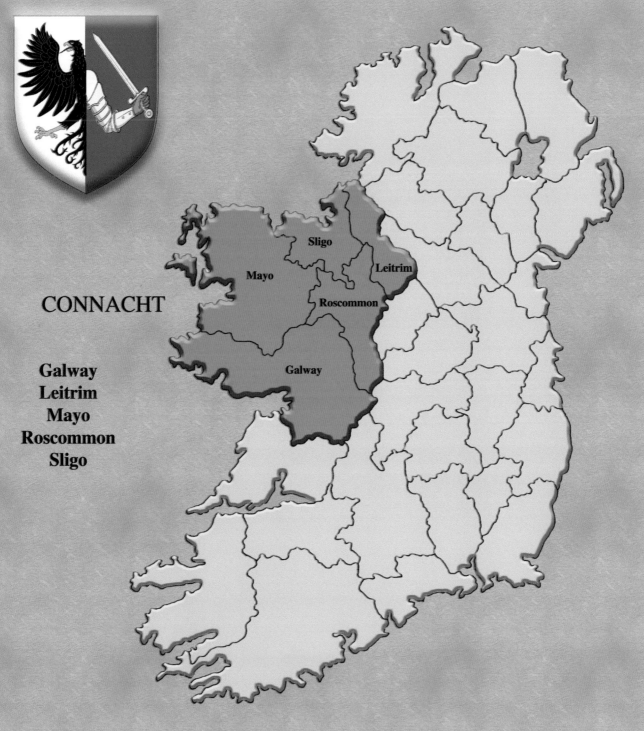

CONNACHT

Galway
Leitrim
Mayo
Roscommon
Sligo

Connacht is a province located in the western part of Ireland known for its rugged landscapes, stunning coastline, and ancient monuments. The region is home to popular ourist attractions such as Connemara National Park, Croagh Patrick, and the Aran Islands.

Antrim (Aontroím)

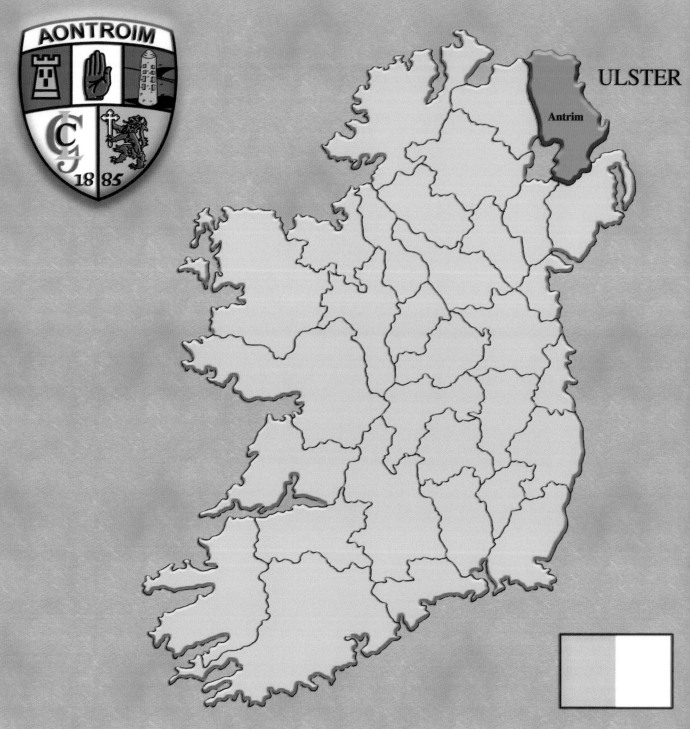

ULSTER

Antrim

County Antrim is in the province of Ulster.
It is the 9th largest county.
The county town is Antrim.
Antrim is known for its stunning coastal scenery, including the
Giant's Causeway and the Glens of Antrim. Other famous landmarks
and attractions include Carrickfergus Castle and the Dark Hedges.

Armagh (Ard Mhacha)

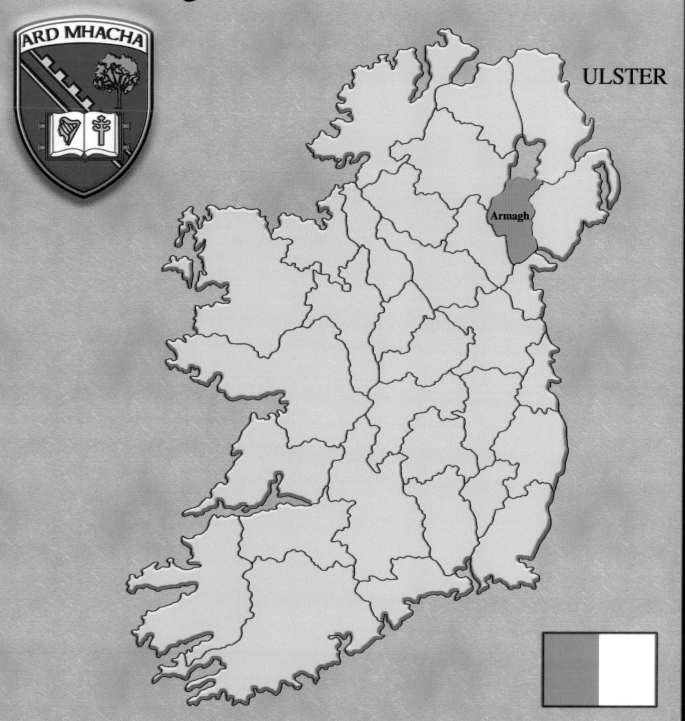

ULSTER

Armagh

County Armagh is in the province of Ulster.
Its is the 27th largest County.
The county town is Armagh city.
It is the ecclesiastical capital of Ireland and is home to two cathedrals.
Other famous landmarks include the Navan Fort and the Armagh Observatory.
The county is also known for its beautiful countryside, including the Ring of Gullion.

Carlow (Ceatharlach)

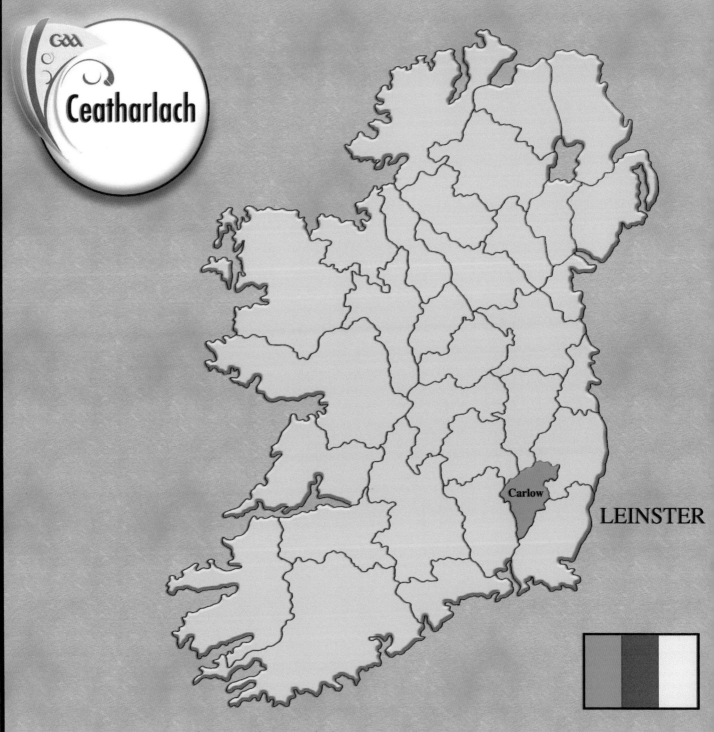

Ceatharlach

Carlow

LEINSTER

County Carlow is in the province of Leinster.
Its is the 31st largest County.
The county town is Carlow town,
Carlow is known for its picturesque landscapes, including the
Blackstairs Mountains and the River Barrow.
Famous landmarks and attractions include Carlow Castle and the Brownshill Dolmen.

Cavan (An Cabhán)

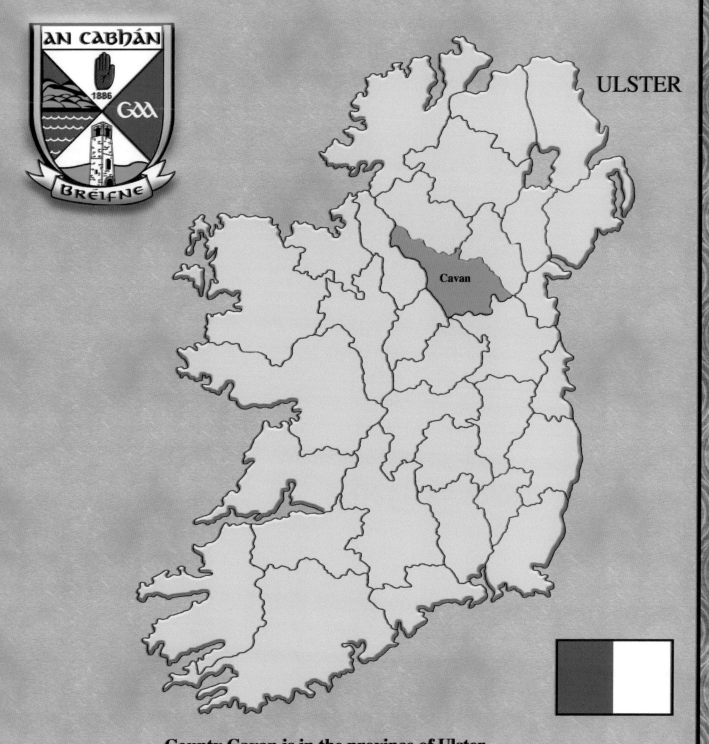

ULSTER

County Cavan is in the province of Ulster.
It is the 19th largest County.
The county town is Cavan town,
It is home to a number of historic landmarks, including Cavan Cathedral,
the Cavan Burren and the Cavan County Museum.
It is known for its scenic beauty, including its lakes, forests, and rolling hills.

Clare (An Clár)

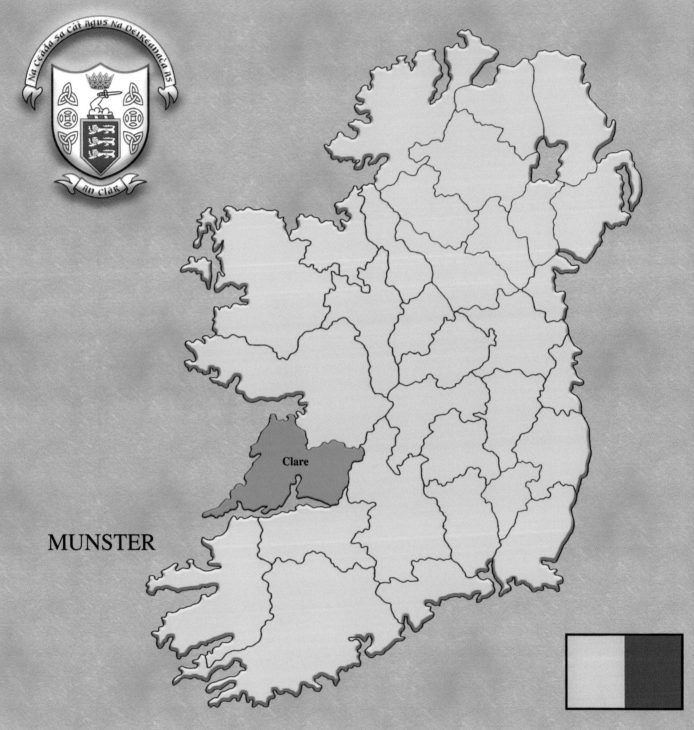

MUNSTER

Clare

County Clare is in the province of Munster.
It is the 7th largest County.
The county town is Ennis.
It is known for its stunning natural beauty,
including the Cliffs of Moher, the Burren, and its coastline.
Other famous landmarks include Bunratty Castle and the Aillwee Cave.

Cork (Corcaigh)

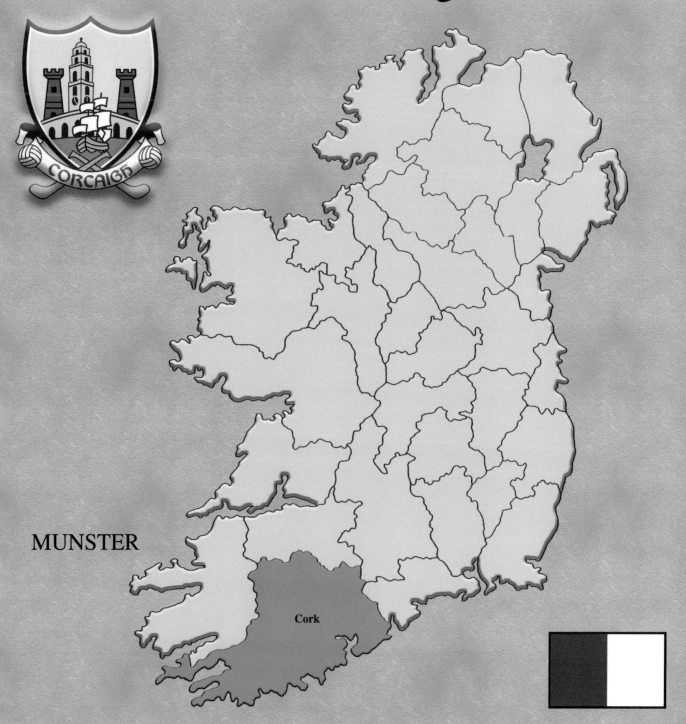

MUNSTER

Cork

County Cork is in the province of Munster.
It is the largest County.
The county town is Cork City.
Cork is known for its stunning coastline, and the Beara Peninsula.
Other famous landmarks and attractions include
Blarney Castle, Fota Wildlife Park, and the English Market

Derry (Doire)

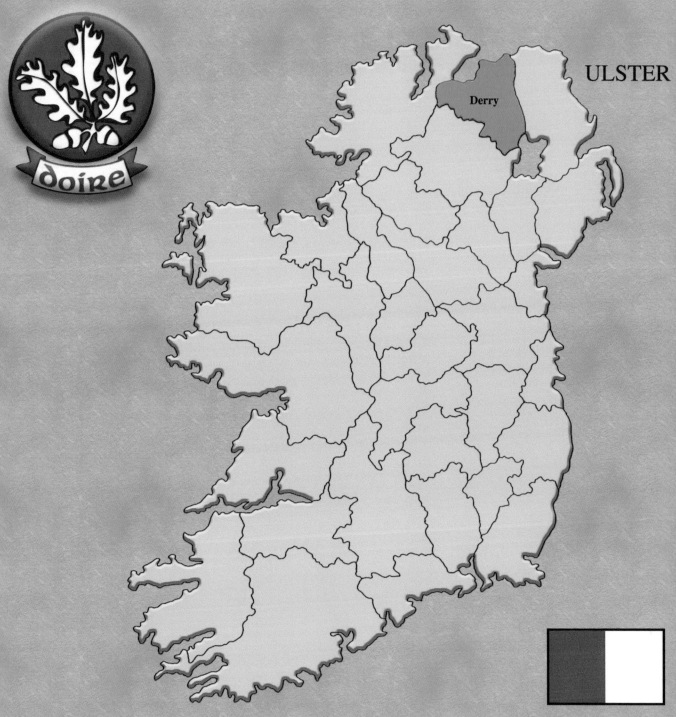

ULSTER

Derry

County Derry is located in the province of Ulster.
It is the 15th largest County.
The county town is Coleraine,
Derry is known for its stunning scenery, including the Sperrin Mountains
and the Causeway Coastal Route. Other famous landmarks and attractions include
the city walls of Derry and the Mussenden Temple.

Donegal (Dhún na nGall)

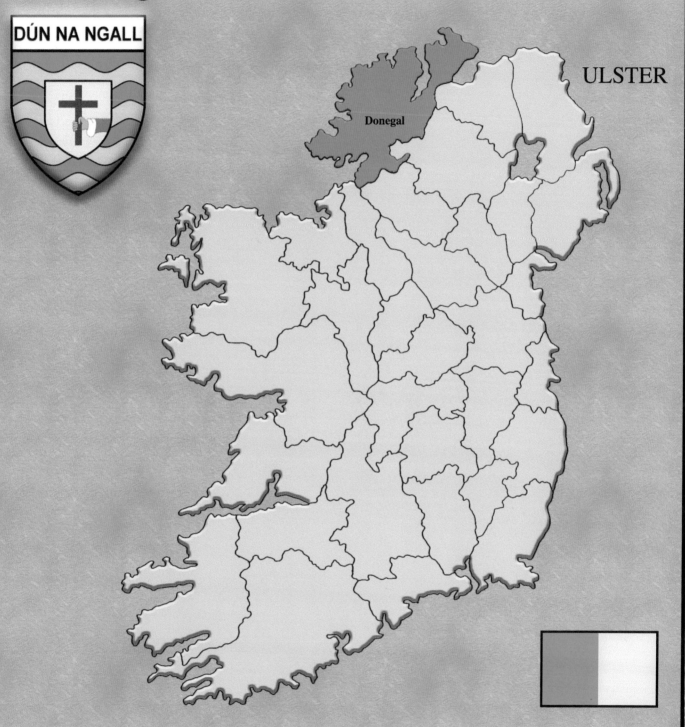

DÚN NA NGALL

ULSTER

Donegal

County Donegal is located in the province of Ulster.
Its is the 4th largest County.
The county town is Lifford.
Donegal is known for its beautiful and rugged coastline, including the Slieve League cliffs
and Glenveagh National Park. Other famous landmarks and attractions include
Malin Head, Fanad Head Lighthouse, and the Inishowen Peninsula.

Down (An Dún)

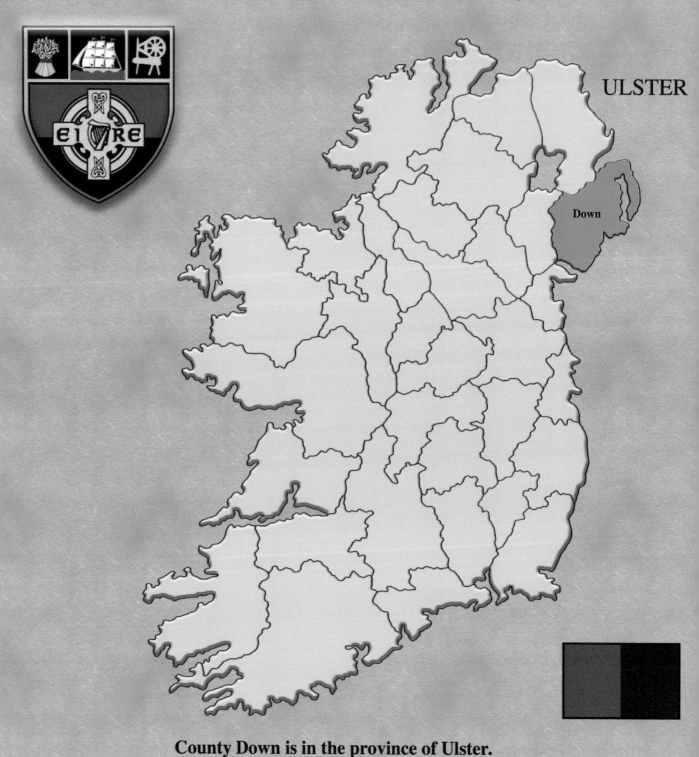

ULSTER

Down

County Down is in the province of Ulster.
Its is the 12th largest County.
The county town is Downpatrick.
Down is known for its stunning natural scenery,
including the Mourne Mountains and Strangford Lough.
Other famous landmarks and attractions include the historic town of
Newry, Castlewellan Forest Park, and Tollymore Forest Park.

Dublin (Baile Átha Cliath)

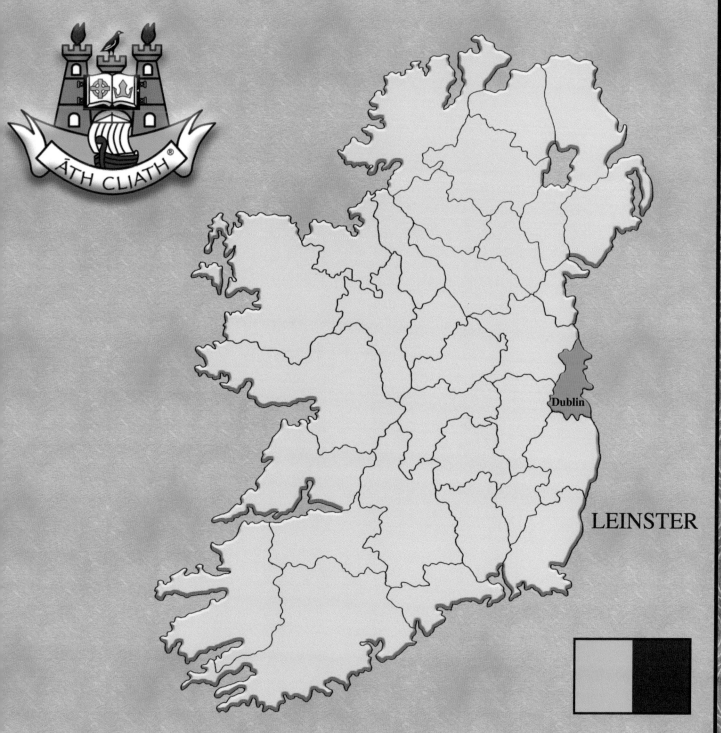

Dublin

LEINSTER

County Dublin is located in the province of Leinster.
It is the 30th largest County.
The old county town is Dublin city, and it is the capital of Ireland.
Dublin is known for its attractions such as Trinity College, Dublin Castle,
and the Guinness Storehouse. The county is also home to many parks,
including Phoenix Park and to many of the country's most important
institutions and landmarks.

Fermanagh (Fear Manach)

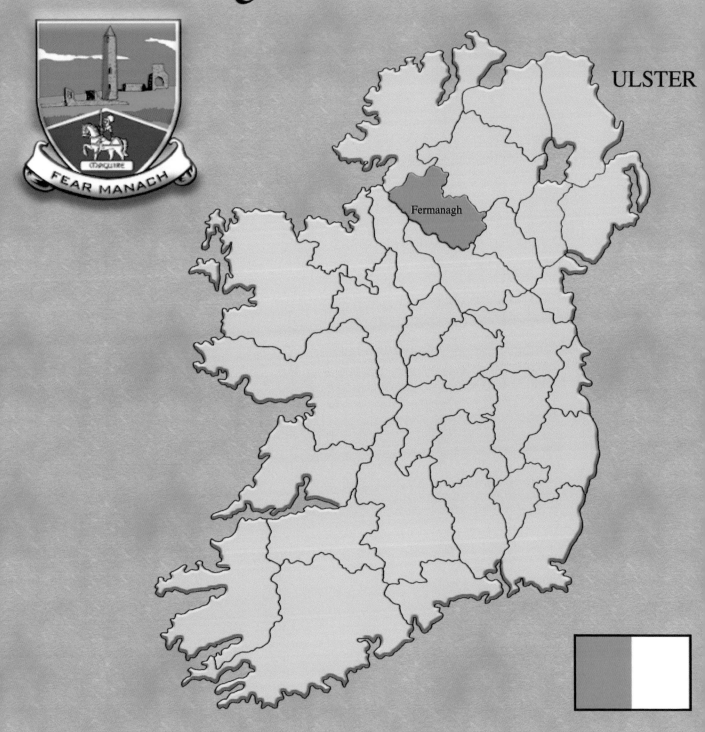

ULSTER

Fermanagh

County Fermanagh is in the province of Ulster.
It is the 25th largest County.
The county town is Enniskillen.
It is known for its picturesque lakelands, including Lough Erne.
Fermanagh is also home to the Marble Arch Caves Global Geopark.
Other famous landmarks and attractions include Enniskillen Castle and Devenish Island.

Galway (Gaillimh)

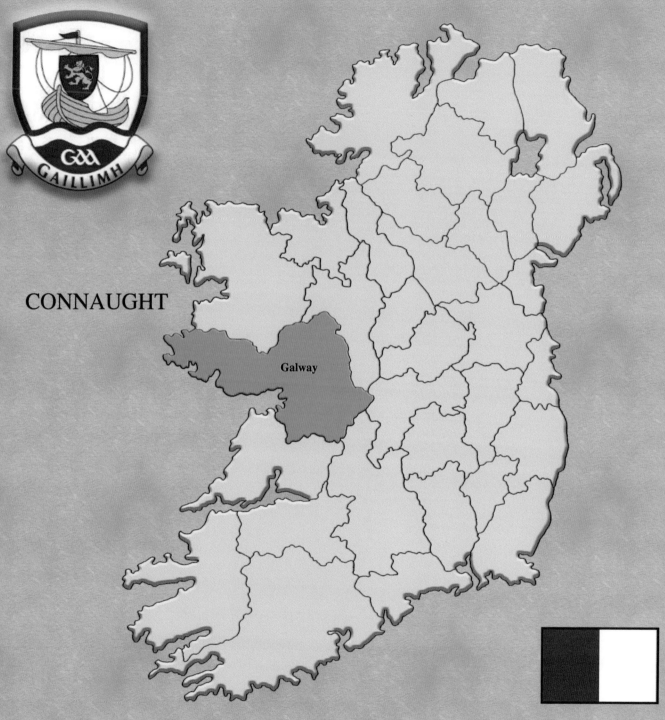

CONNAUGHT

Galway

County Galway is in the province of Connacht.
It is the 2nd largest County.
The county town is Galway city.
It is a popular tourist destination known for its medieval architecture,
traditional Irish music, and Connemara National Park.
It is known for its rugged coastline, beautiful countryside, and vibrant cultural scene.

Kerry (Cíarraí)

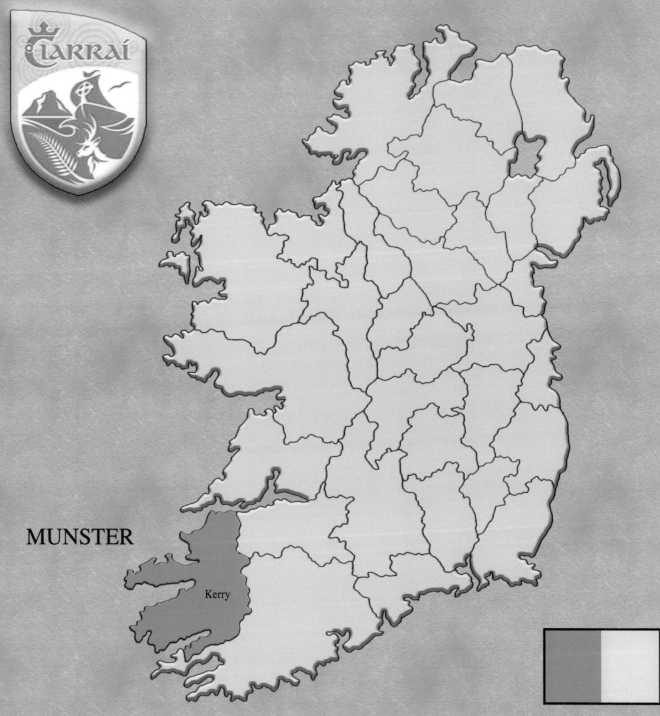

MUNSTER

Kerry

County Kerry is in the province of Munster.
It is the 5th largest County.
The county town is Tralee.
It is known for its stunning natural beauty,
including the Ring of Kerry scenic drive, the Dingle Peninsula,
Carrauntoohil - the highest mountain in Ireland and the Killarney National Park

Kildare (Cill Dara)

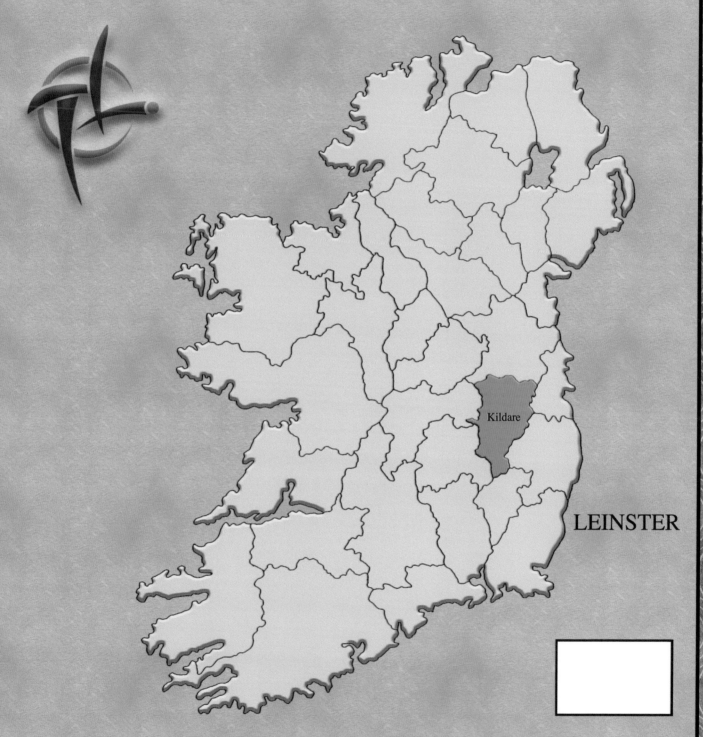

Kildare

LEINSTER

**County Kildare is in the province of Leinster.
It is the 24th largest county.
The county town is Naas.
Kildare is known for its horse racing, with the famous Curragh and Punchestown
racecourses located in the county. Other famous landmarks and attractions include
the Irish National Stud and the Castletown House estate.**

Kilkenny (Cill Chainnigh)

Cill Chainnigh

LEINSTER

Kilkenny

County Kilkenny is in the province of Leinster.
It is the 16th largest county.
The county town is Kilkenny.
Kilkenny is known for its medieval history and architecture, including Kilkenny Castle,
St. Canice's Cathedral, and the Kilkenny City Walls. Other popular attractions include
the Smithwick's Brewery, the Black Abbey, and the Rothe House and Gardens.

Laois (Laois)

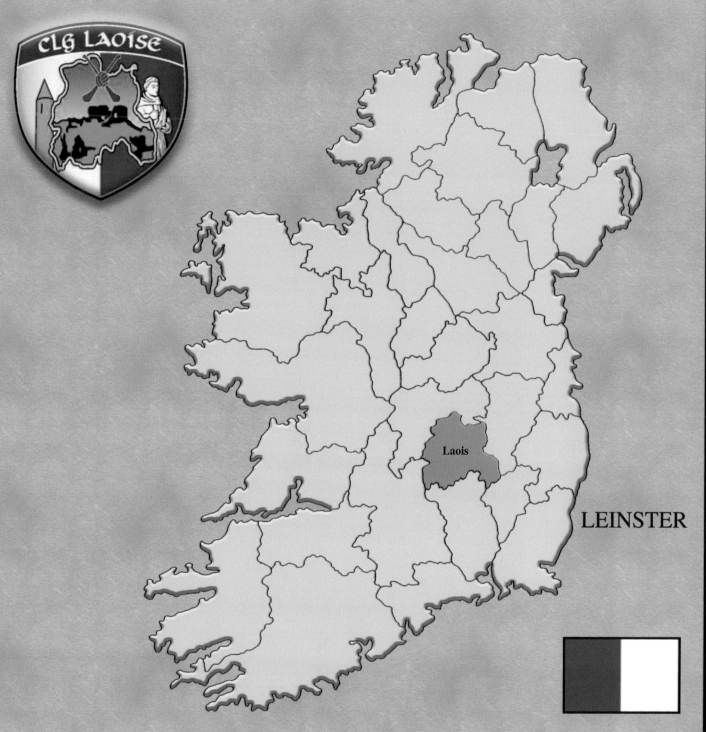

LEINSTER

Laois

County Laois is in the province of Leinster.
It is the 23rd largest county.
The county town is Portlaoise.
Laois is known for its beautiful landscapes, including the Slieve Bloom Mountains
and the River Barrow. Other famous landmarks and attractions include
Emo Court House and Gardens, the Rock
of Dunamase and the ruins of the medieval Dunamase Castle.

Leitrim (Liatroim)

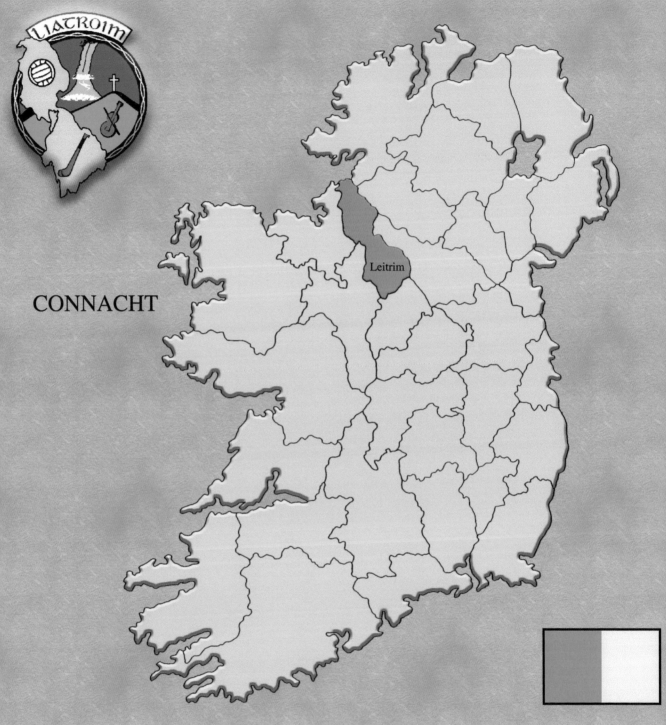

CONNACHT

Leitrim

County Leitrim is in the province of Connacht.
It is the 26th largest County.
The county town is Carrick-on-Shannon.
The River Shannon, the longest river in Ireland, runs through the county
and there are many historic sites and cultural attractions to explore.
Including the 12th-century Creevelea Abbey and the Glencar Waterfall.

Limerick (Luimneach)

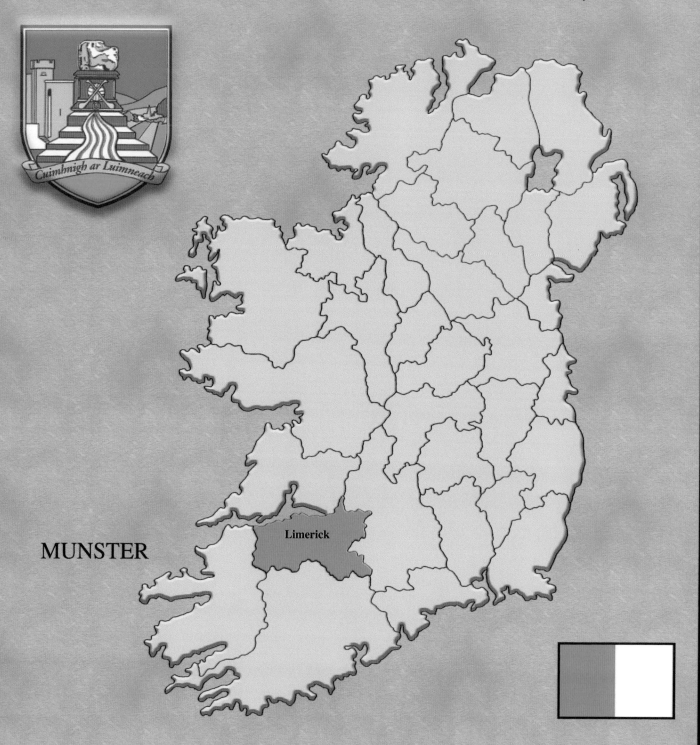

MUNSTER

Limerick

County Limerick is in the province of Munster.
It is the 10th largest county.
The county town is Limerick City.
Limerick is known for its historic castles, such as King John's Castle, Adare Castle
and the medieval St. Mary's Cathedral. Other famous
landmarks include the Foynes Flying Boat and Maritime Museum.

Longford (An Longfort)

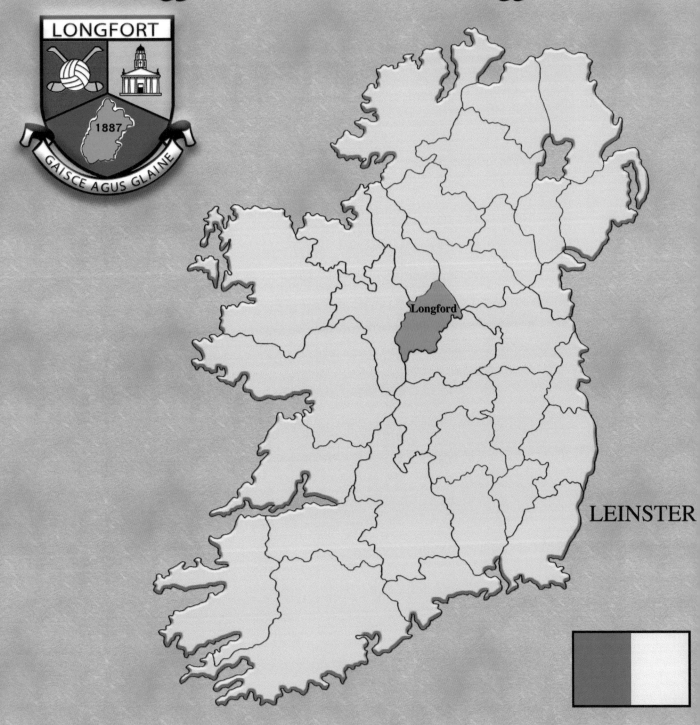

LEINSTER

County Longford is in the province of Leinster.
It is the 29th largest county.
The county town is Longford.
Longford is known for its tranquil countryside, lakes, and rivers.
Other notable attractions include the Corlea Trackway Visitor Centre,
the Royal Canal Greenway and the ancient monastic settlement of Ardagh

Louth (Lú)

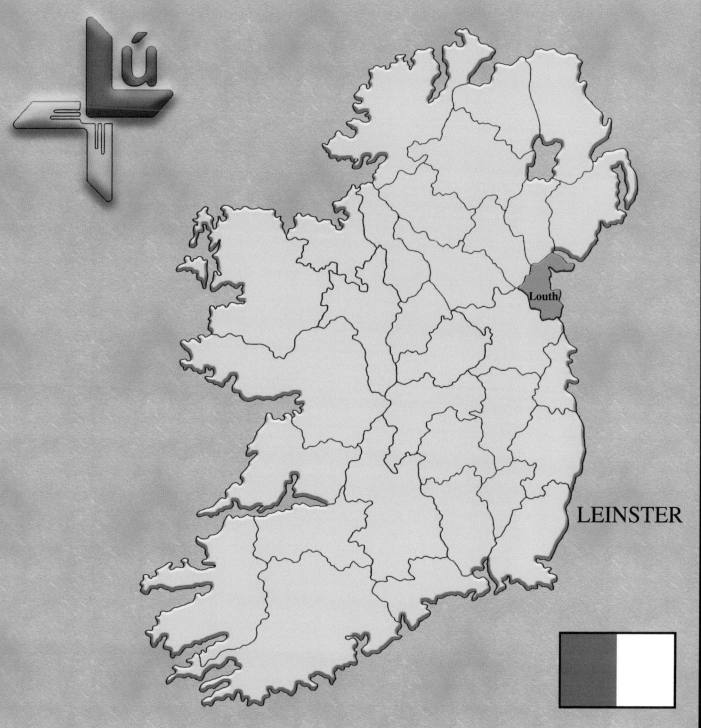

LEINSTER

County Louth is in the province of Leinster.
It is the smallest county.
The county town is Dundalk.
Louth is known for its rich history and heritage, including the ancient
monastic site of Monasterboice and the legendary tale of Cuchulainn.
Other famous landmarks include the Cooley Mountains and Carlingford Lough.

Mayo (Maigh Eo)

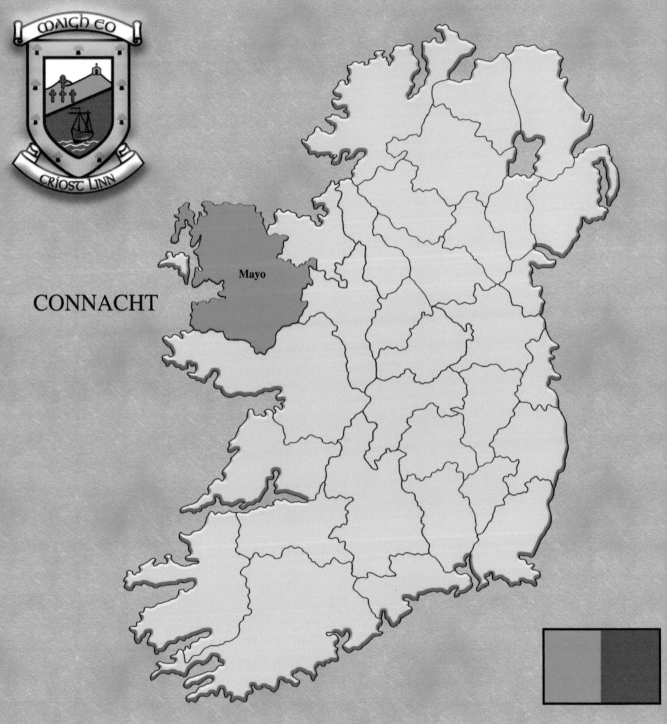

CONNACHT

County Mayo is in the province of Connacht.
It is the 3rd largest county.
The county town is Castlebar.
Mayo has a rugged and varied landscape, including the Atlantic Ocean,
mountains, and plains.
Famous landmarks and attractions include Croagh Patrick and the Ceide Fields.

Meath (An Mhí)

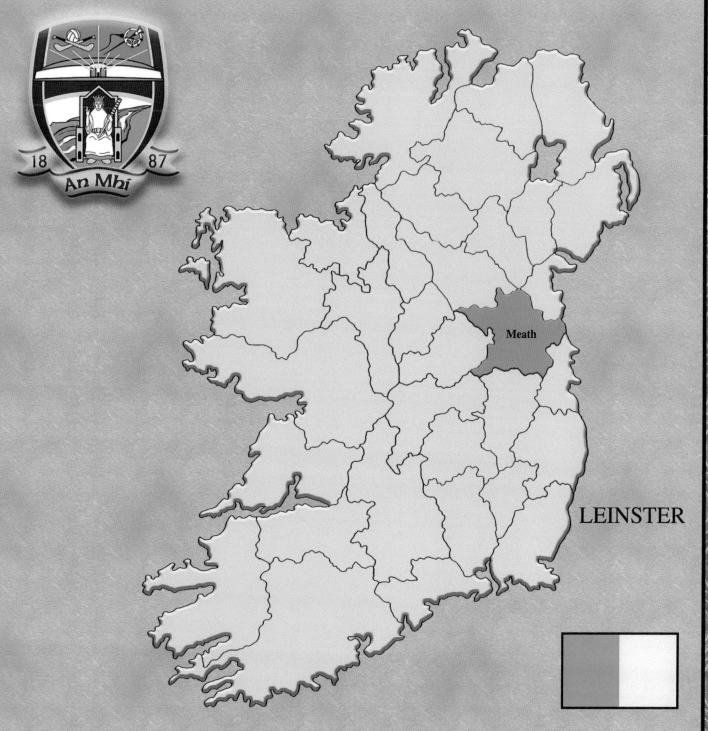

Meath

LEINSTER

County Meath is in the province of Leinster.
It is the 14th largest county.
The county town is Navan.
Meath is known for its rich history, including the ancient sites of
Newgrange, Knowth, and Dowth.
Other famous landmarks and attractions include the Hill of Tara and Trim Castle.

Monaghan (Muineachán)

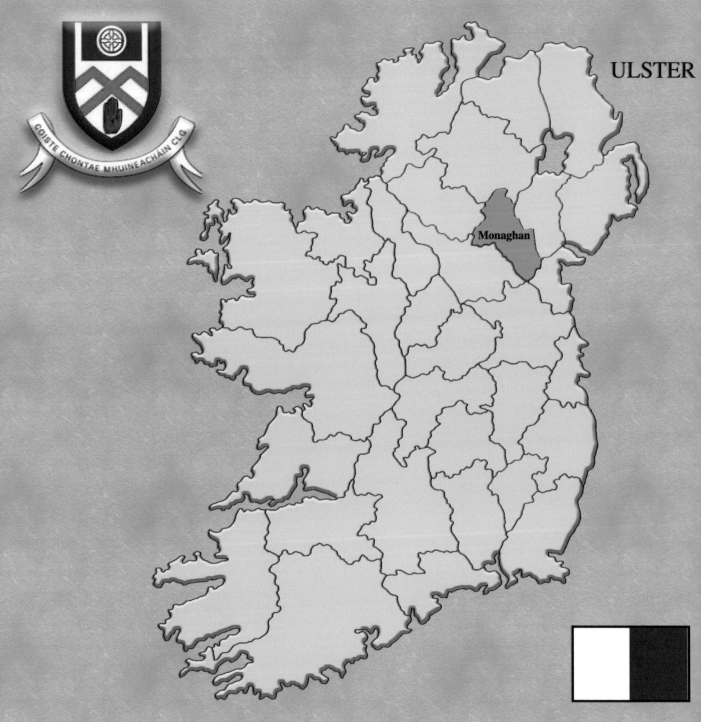

ULSTER

Monaghan

County Monaghan is in the province of Ulster.
It is the 28th largest county.
The county town is Monaghan.
Monaghan is known for its scenic countryside and lakes. Famous landmarks include
the Castle Leslie estate, the Patrick Kavanagh Centre and the medieval
Round Tower of Clones and the 19th-century Rossmore Forest Park

Offaly (Uibh Fhailí)

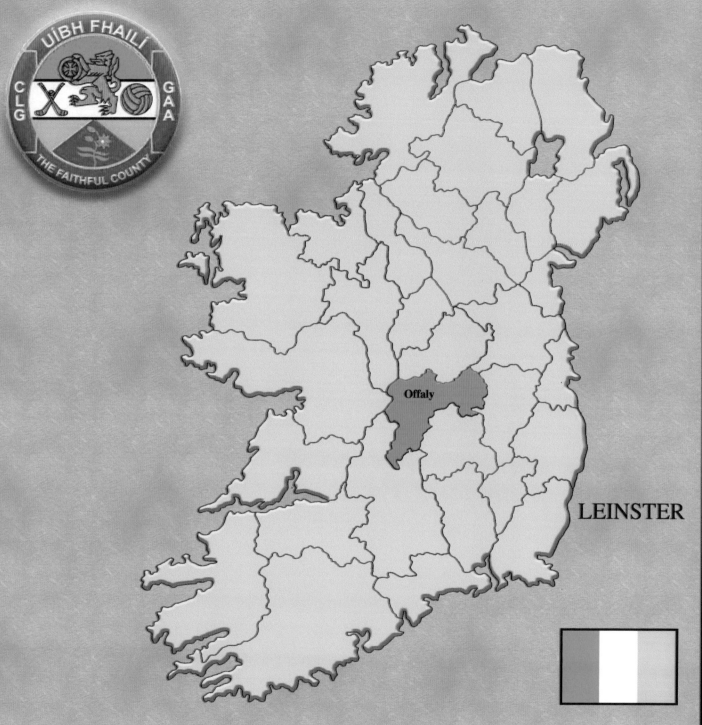

Offaly

LEINSTER

County Offaly is in the province of Leinster.
It is the 18th largest county.
The county town is Tullamore.
Offaly is known for its lush countryside, including the Slieve Bloom Mountains and
the Grand Canal. Famous landmarks and attractions include
the ancient monastic settlement of Clonmacnoise and Birr Castle.

Roscommon (Ros Comáin)

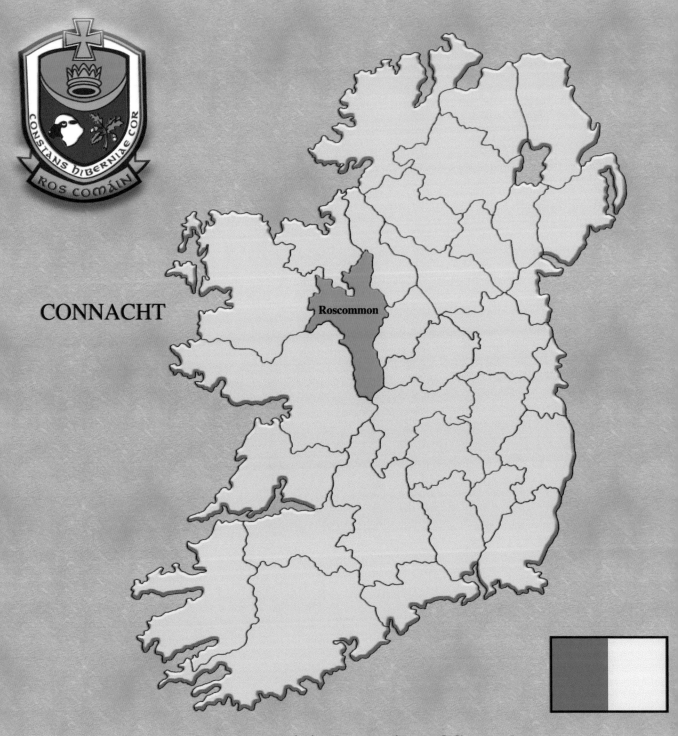

CONNACHT

Roscommon

**County Roscommon is in the province of Connacht.
It is the 11th largest county.
The county town is Roscommon.
Roscommon is known for its unspoiled natural beauty, with vast forests, rolling hills,
and picturesque lakes. Famous landmarks include the Lough Key Forest
and Activity Park, the Arigna Mining Experience, and Boyle Abbey.**

Sligo (Sligeach)

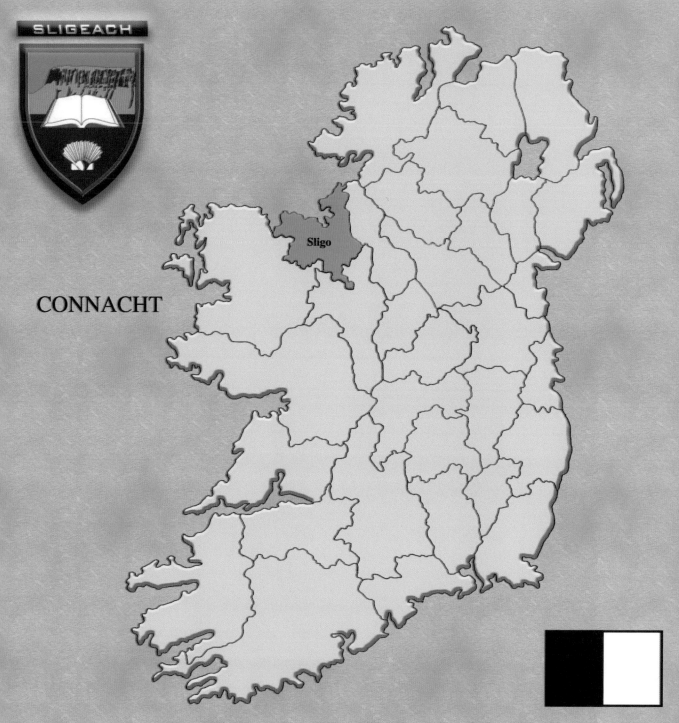

SLIGEACH

CONNACHT

Sligo

County Sligo is in the province of Connacht.
It is the 22nd largest county.
The county town is Sligo.
Sligo is known for its beautiful beaches, including Rosses Point and Strandhill.
Other famous landmarks and attractions include
Ben Bulben and the megalithic cemetery at Carrowmore.

Tipperary (Tiobraid Árann)

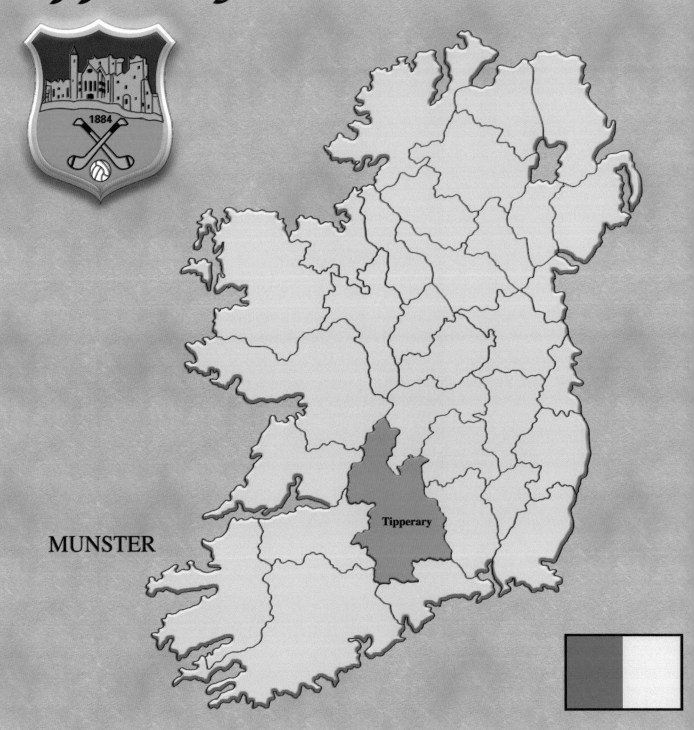

MUNSTER

Tipperary

County Tipperary is in the province of Munster.
It is the 6th largest county.
The county towns are Clonmel/Nenagh.
Tipperary is known for its scenic countryside, including the Galtee Mountains
and the Glen of Aherlow. Other famous landmarks and attractions include
the Rock of Cashel and Cahir Castle.

Tyrone (Tír Eoghain)

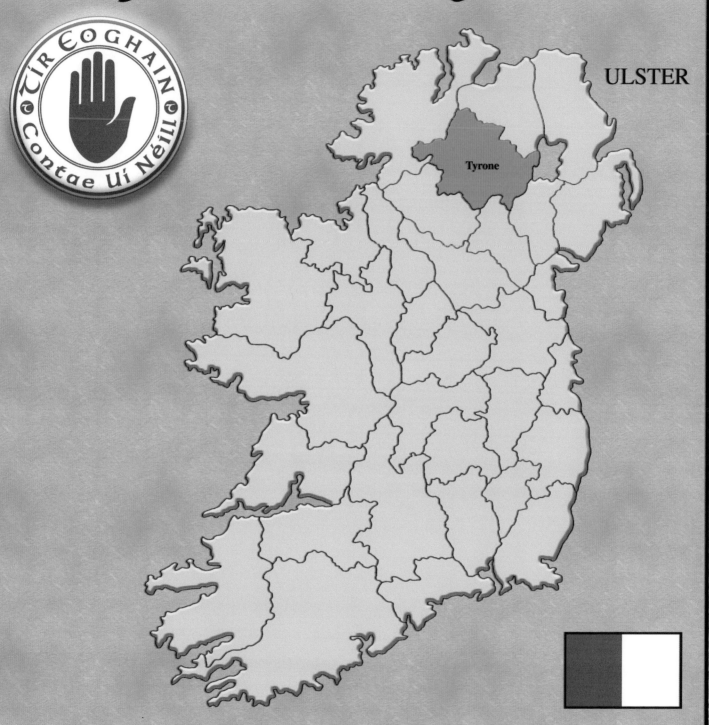

ULSTER

Tyrone

County Tyrone is in the province of Ulster.
It is the 8th largest county.
The county town is Omagh.
Tyrone has a rich history and is home to many important sites,
including the Ulster American Folk Park, the Beaghmore Stone Circles,
the Gortin Glen Forest Park and the ruins of the 16th-century Omagh Castle.

Waterford (Port Láirge)

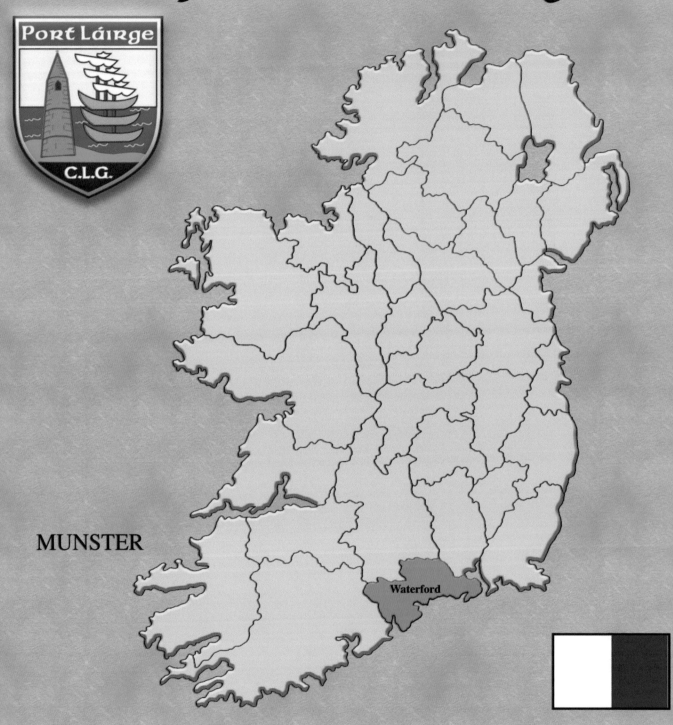

MUNSTER

County Waterford is in the province of Munster.
It is the 20th largest county.
The county town is Dungarvan.
Waterford is home to the historic Waterford Crystal factory and showroom.
Other famous landmarks and attractions include the
Copper Coast Geopark, Lismore Castle Gardens and Reginald's Tower.

Westmeath (An Iarmhí)

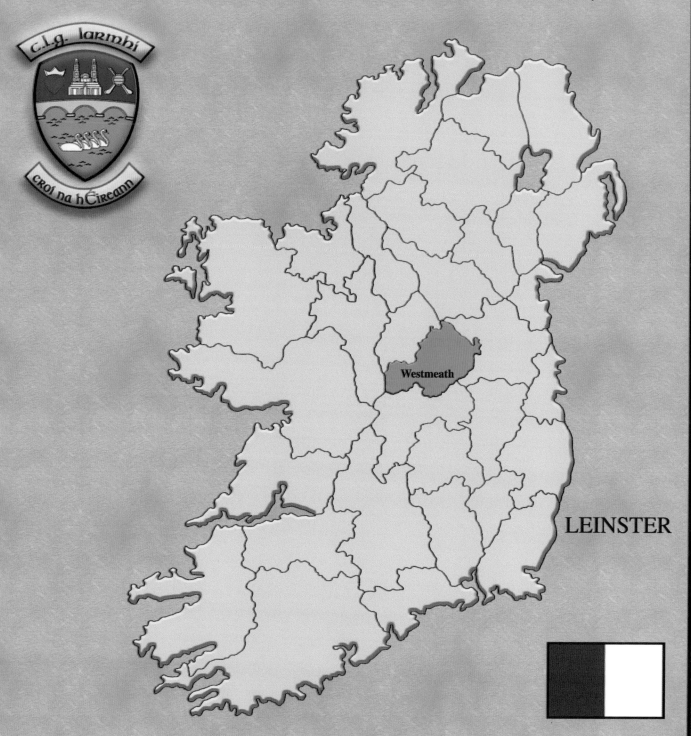

LEINSTER

Westmeath

County Westmeath is in the province of Leinster.
It is the 21st largest county.
The county town is Mullingar.
Westmeath is known for its beautiful lakes, including Lough Ennell, Lough Owel,
and Lough Derravaragh. Other famous landmarks and attractions include
the Belvedere House and Gardens and the Hill of Uisneach.

Wexford (Loch Garman)

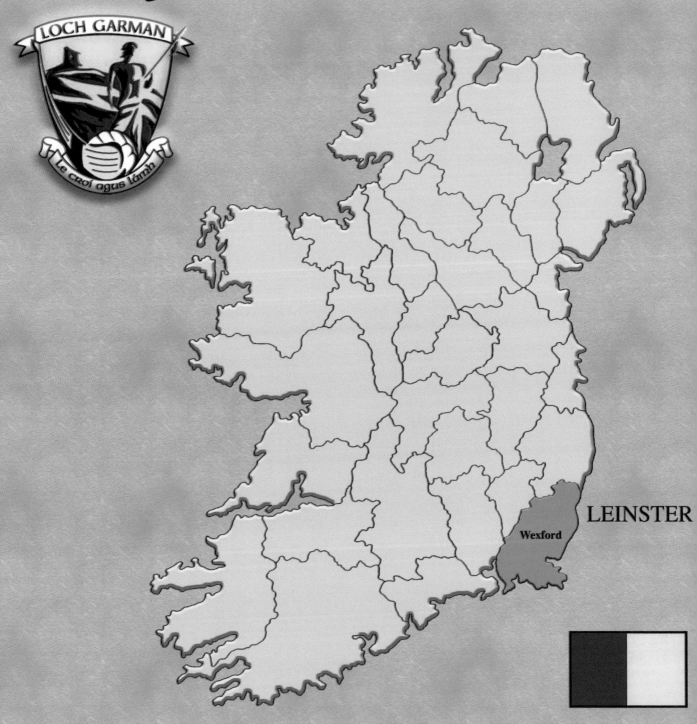

LEINSTER

Wexford

County Wexford is in the province of Leinster.
It is the 13th largest county.
The county town is Wexford.
Wexford is known for its beautiful beaches and coastline, including Curracloe Beach
Other famous landmarks and attractions include the Hook Lighthouse,
the Irish National Heritage Park, and the Dunbrody Famine Ship.

Wicklow (Cill Mhantáin)

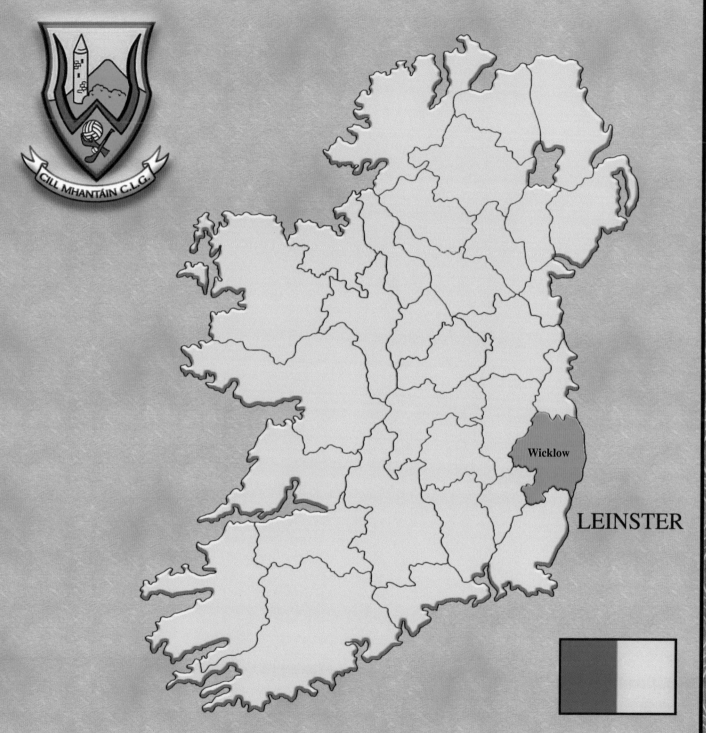

LEINSTER

County Wicklow is in the province of Leinster.
It is the 17th largest county.
The county town is Wicklow.
Wicklow is known as the "Garden of Ireland" due to its beautiful natural scenery.
Famous landmarks and attractions include
Glendalough, the Wicklow Mountains, and the Wicklow Way hiking trail.

Ireland

ULSTER

Donegal

Derry

Antrim

Tyrone

Fermanagh

Down

Armagh

Monaghan

Sligo

Leitrim

Cavan

CONNACHT

Mayo

Roscommon

Longford

Louth

Meath

Galway

Westmeath

Offaly

Dublin

Kildare

Laois

Wicklow

Clare

Carlow

LEINSTER

Limerick

Tipperary

Kilkenny

Wexford

MUNSTER

Kerry

Waterford

Cork

An té a bhíonn siúlach, bíonn sé scéalach.
(He who travels has stories to tell.)

Printed in Great Britain
by Amazon

20768549R00027